LIBERTY AND JUSTICE

THE SILENT SENTINELS

BY JASON NORD

RESISTANCE
TO TYRANNY
IS OBEDIENCE
TO GOD.

America was a different place back in 1917. People didn't have the same rights that we enjoy today. If you were a woman, you were not supposed to become a doctor or a lawyer, a firefighter or an athlete, a scientist or a philosopher. You were not expected to have great ideas that could change the world, and if you did, you certainly weren't supposed to share them with anyone else. The truth is, if you were a woman in America back in 1917, you were expected to have babies, keep the house clean, stay quiet, and keep your opinions to yourself.

But all of this was changing. Since the middle of the 1800s, a small group of women had been raising their voices, demanding the same rights that the men in America enjoyed. They wanted the right to own property, the right to have an education, the right to stand up in public and share their ideas with the rest of society. Some of these women – people who called themselves suffragists – focused their attention on one right in particular.

They wanted the right to vote.

Many men were opposed to the idea of women voting. They believed that women weren't smart enough to make decisions for themselves, and that if women had the right to vote, they would just copy their husbands, fathers, or brothers.

Other men were just downright afraid. They argued that if women could vote, they'd take over the entire government. Others feared that women's suffrage would somehow destroy the country or even cause all of the nations of the world to collapse. Men were used to having all of the power in society. For some of them, the idea of having to share that power was terrifying.

For decades, suffragists had been asking politely for the men in power to give them the right to vote. For decades, the men in power – the president and those in the Senate and the House of Representatives – had ignored them.

One group of suffragists – women who called themselves the Silent Sentinels – was tired of being ignored.

It started in Washington DC on a frigid day near the beginning of January. Twelve women marched out of the front doors of the Cameron House, the building that served as the headquarters for a suffragist group called the National Woman's Party. They wore thick dresses, coats, and hats to protect themselves from the winter cold. Across their chests, each of the women wore a sash striped with purple, white, and gold – the colors of the suffragist movement. In their hands they grasped long wooden poles that carried banners, signs, and flags. In their minds, these women viewed themselves as peaceful soldiers, "the embodiment of a gigantic army" that was "waging a war for peace, for right and equality."

Their destination was the White House. Just the day before, suffragists from the National Woman's Party had met with President Woodrow Wilson. They had asked him to support the Susan B. Anthony Amendment, a proposed change to the United States Constitution that would guarantee women in America the right to vote.

Wilson had turned them down. In the middle of their meeting, he had left the room and closed the door behind him. He wasn't interested in promoting women's suffrage.

And so the Silent Sentinels were born.

When the women reached the White House, they positioned themselves around the two main gates. There they unfurled their banners. One of them read:

MR. PRESIDENT, WHAT WILL YOU DO FOR WOMAN SUFFRAGE?

Another one asked:

MR. PRESIDENT, HOW LONG MUST WOMEN WAIT FOR LIBERTY?

Those first Sentinels stood in front of the White House for four hours. They shivered from the cold, and their feet grew sore from standing. At around one in the afternoon, another group came from the Cameron House to replace the first group. Those women also took a four-hour shift.

The Sentinels' plan was to return to the White House every day, keeping watch over the front gates. They would make sure that the president couldn't ignore them. Every time that he left his house and every time that he returned home, the Silent Sentinels would be waiting there for him. Every person who visited the president would see the Sentinels' signs and realize that Woodrow Wilson was standing in the way of women's equality. The Sentinels would be peaceful, they would be patient, they would be persistent, and they would be heard.

Day after day, the suffragists returned. The winter was cold that year, yet no matter the weather – driving rain, savage winds, or blowing snow – the Silent Sentinels maintained their posts. Supporters would bring them hot bricks to stand on to keep their feet warm and thermoses of coffee to ward away the cold. Several of the suffragists developed frostbite, while others fell ill from the long hours spent standing outside in the winter weather.

Newspaper reporters from across the country wrote stories about the Sentinels, though many of them had only bad things to say. Nobody in the history of the country had ever protested in front of the White House, and some people found it shocking or immoral. The *New York Times* called the suffragists "silly" and "offensive." But others were inspired by the Silent Sentinels. Women from around the United States decided to travel to Washington DC and join the Sentinels in their quest for equality and justice.

DEMOCRACY
SHOULD BEGIN
AT HOME

The days turned into weeks, the weeks turned into months, and still the Sentinels gathered, maintaining their watch over the White House.

In early April, 1917, President Wilson announced that America would be joining World War One. He delivered grand speeches about how American men needed to fight for democracy in foreign countries. The suffragists viewed him as a hypocrite – someone who says one thing, but does another. In their eyes, Wilson was willing to talk about the beauty of democracy in his speeches, but he was unwilling to make America a true democracy, a place where everyone, men and women, could make decisions together as equals.

And so they used his words against him.

The Sentinels began carrying banners that quoted President Wilson. One of their signs read:

Then on June 20, 1917, the violence started.

A group of people from the Russian government was visiting the White House that day. Russia was a democracy in 1917, and Russian women had the right to vote. When the Silent Sentinels approached the White House gates that morning, they brought with them a banner that carried a message for the Russian government. It proclaimed:

WE, THE WOMEN OF AMERICA, TELL YOU THAT AMERICA IS NOT A DEMOCRACY. TWENTY MILLION AMERICAN WOMEN ARE DENIED THE RIGHT TO VOTE.

Near its end, the banner read:

HELP US MAKE THIS NATION REALLY FREE. TELL OUR GOVERNMENT THAT IT MUST LIBERATE THE PEOPLE BEFORE IT CAN CLAIM FREE RUSSIA AS AN ALLY.

An angry crowd began to gather in the streets. Government workers, free on their lunch breaks, swarmed around the White House gates, forming a mob of several hundred people. They surrounded the suffragists, shouting insults at them and calling them traitors. One man yelled, "Come on, boys, let's tear that thing down!" Then he pulled out a knife. Leaping forward, he slashed the banner and tore it from its poles. He and another man ripped it to shreds.

The next day, the Sentinels returned with a banner identical to the one that the men had destroyed. This time, a mob of more than a thousand people gathered and attacked the suffragists. They tore up the women's banners and smashed the poles to pieces. The crowd spat at the suffragists, yanked their hair, and dragged them to the ground.

Throughout this, the Silent Sentinels remained peaceful. Though they were afraid, they stayed brave and they stayed strong. They knew that what they were doing was right and that their message needed to be heard.

That night, the superintendent of police, a man named Raymond Pullman, went to the Cameron House. He demanded to speak with a woman named Alice Paul. Paul was one of the cofounders of the National Woman's Party and a leader of the Silent Sentinels. Pullman ordered Paul to make the protests stop. He told her that any women caught picketing in front of the White House would be arrested.

Alice knew that the Sentinels were not breaking the law, that they had the right to gather in public and peacefully express their beliefs. But she also knew that if somebody in power, such as President Wilson or the district attorney, wanted the Sentinels arrested, then it would happen whether the women were breaking the law or not.

With determination in her eyes, Alice Paul looked at Superintendent Pullman and gave him her response:

"The picketing will go on as usual."

Alice Paul

The next morning, police officers gathered outside the Cameron House, ready to arrest any women who dared to picket the president's home.   Three brave suffragists – Lucy Burns, Katherine Morey, and Mabel Vernon – managed to sneak past the police officers with a banner.

Mabel Vernon

Katharine Morey

They proudly took their position in front of the east gates of the White House and unfurled their message. It was the quote from President Wilson's speech about the importance of fighting for democracy.

When the police realized what had happened, they swooped in to grab the three suffragists. Mabel Vernon managed to escape, but Lucy Burns and Katherine Morey were arrested for obstructing traffic.

Lucy Burns

Day after day this scene repeated itself. Silent Sentinels appeared before the White House gates, flags and banners gripped tightly in their hands. Then the police came and arrested them.

Meanwhile, mobs of angry men continued to gather in the streets, harassing and attacking the suffragists. The men threw fruit and eggs at the Sentinels. They hit them, choked them, and dragged them across the sidewalks. They stole the suffragists' banners and destroyed them.

One day in August, a group of men attacked the Cameron House itself. They brought ladders to scale the outside walls to tear down flags and banners from the balcony. Somebody in the mob fired a pistol through one of the front windows; the bullet almost hit one of the Sentinels in the head.

While all of this was happening, the police just sat back and watched. They allowed men to attack the suffragists, then after a while the police would grab the women and arrest them for blocking traffic. The people who were truly breaking the law – the men who were attacking innocent people – were ignored or even encouraged by the police. Meanwhile the Silent Sentinels – women who wanted nothing but to speak out for liberty and justice – were arrested and taken to jail.

Life inside of the jails was horrible for the arrested suffragists. Their cells were cold, wet, and dirty, crawling with bedbugs, cockroaches, and rats. Because the guards wouldn't give them proper blankets, the women began wrapping themselves in old newspapers, trying desperately to stay warm. Their meals consisted of rotting meat, moldy bread, and corn-meal mush infested with worms, mouse feces, and dead flies. Many of the women became sick from the disgusting food. Dudley Field Malone, a former friend to President Wilson who had quit his government job to act as a lawyer for the Silent Sentinels, described the conditions of the jails as "rotten," "filthy," and "depraved."

Yet no matter what happened, the Sentinels kept going. They continued their vigil in front of the White House gates, knowing that they would likely be attacked, arrested, and thrown into a prison cell. Many of them were sent to jail more than once; Lucy Burns was arrested six different times for protesting in front of the president's home. But for the Sentinels it was worth it; they knew that the world would never improve if people weren't willing to stand up and struggle for a better future.

Then, on October 20, Alice Paul was arrested and sentenced to seven months in the district jail for blocking the sidewalk. At first, her supporters would come to stand outside the window of her cell. They yelled things like, "Oklahoma is with you!" or, "New York salutes you!" to show that there were people from across the country who supported the Silent Sentinels. But the jail keepers didn't like this. They moved Alice to a new cell and boarded all of the windows shut, leaving her in darkness, separated from the outside world.

While in jail, Alice Paul and another suffragist named Rose Winslow decided to continue their protest. The government had taken away all of their rights, but the two suffragists still had one way to show their determination: they decided to stop eating. If the government was going to treat them horrendously simply because they had asked for the right to vote, then the women would starve themselves to make their point. They were willing to give up their own lives so that other women could live in a world with equality.

Rose Winslow

People in the government were afraid. They knew that if suffragists started dying while in jail that people around the world would hear about it, that they would be outraged, and that the suffrage movement would grow stronger. So government officials decided to start forcing the suffragists to eat.

Three times a day, Alice and Rose were taken from their cells. While several men held them down, a rubber tube was forced up their noses, down their throats, and into their stomachs. Liquid food was then poured into the tube and directly into their bodies.

This process was very painful. Rose Winslow reported that she wept after every one of her forced feedings.

Still, the women stayed strong. One of the jail's workers, seeing Alice's determination, described her this way:

"She will die, but she will never give up."

In early November, while Alice and Rose were locked in the city's district jail, around forty other Sentinels were arrested and taken to the Occoquan Workhouse in Virginia. When they arrived, the suffragists refused to go to their cells until they were guaranteed healthy food, clean clothes, and the right to read books and newspapers while in their cells. The prison guards reacted violently. And so began what the suffragists would later name the Night of Terror.

Lucy Burns

Vida Milholland

The women were dragged and pushed through the dark, dungeon-like hallways of Occoquan. They were thrown to the ground and slammed against metal furniture. A Sentinel named Dora Lewis described hearing the sounds of "shrieks, cries," and "heavy bodies falling." When Lucy Burns began calling out her friends' names, trying to make sure that everyone was safe, the guards handcuffed her to the bars of her cell with her arms hanging above her head.

The next morning, when the violence was over, it would have been easy for the Sentinels to give up. Instead, they announced that, like Alice Paul and Rose Winslow, they too would refuse to eat. They would rather starve to death in prison than live in a world where women's rights were completely ignored by the government.

As they had done with Alice and Rose, the prison guards began force feeding the women three times a day.

the Sentinels. The suffragists in Occoquan managed to smuggle secret messages out of the prison, describing the abuses that they suffered, and the National Woman's Party mailed out thousands of letters to people throughout the country, informing them of the horrible conditions that the suffragists experienced in jail.

Meanwhile, volunteers from the National Woman's Party toured the country giving speeches about the work of the Silent Sentinels. Dressed in prison uniforms, they told large crowds of men and women about the suffering endured by the arrested suffragists. In Pensacola, Florida, three hundred people showed up to hear the Sentinels' tale. More than a thousand people attended a rally in Mobile, Alabama. These speeches were met with thunderous applause, and the people who saw them left determined to help in the struggle.

Letters and telegrams from men and women across the country began flooding into the White House, demanding that the Sentinels be released from jail and that women be given the right to vote. Even Woodrow Wilson's friends and allies began urging him to give in to the Sentinels' demands for equality.

The president found himself in a tough situation. He wanted the country to be united behind his war effort, but instead the country was divided, arguing about women's suffrage. And as the days and weeks passed, more and more people became angry with the president because of how the Sentinels were being treated. Wilson had hoped that the suffragists would just quietly disappear, but instead the cry for women's equality grew louder every day.

On November 23, the suffragists from Occoquan were brought into a Washington DC courtroom. They were battered, tired, and dirty; several of them were too weak to stand and used their coats to make beds on the hard wooden benches. They told their stories to the judge, and Dudley Field Malone, acting as their lawyer, argued that the government was acting illegally and that the suffragists should be set free. The judge listened patiently. He spent three days considering the arguments. Finally he declared that the women's treatment in jail had been "blood-curdling." He ordered the government to release all of the Silent Sentinels at once.

Around this time, Alice Paul received a visit from a man named David Lawrence, a journalist and close friend to Woodrow Wilson. He came to her cell secretly in the middle of the night. He suggested that if the Sentinels would agree to end their protests, thereby leaving the president alone, Wilson would begin taking steps to pass the Susan B. Anthony Amendment, giving women the right to vote. We don't know what Alice Paul said back to David Lawrence, but we do know what she did next.

It was November 28, 1917. Alice Paul was being released from jail. She had lost a lot of weight during her imprisonment, but she was just as determined as ever to fight for women's equality. When reporters asked her if the protests would continue, Alice looked at them and said, "We hope that no more demonstrations will be necessary. But what we do depends entirely upon what the administration does." In other words, the Silent Sentinels would be watching. If Woodrow Wilson began helping suffragists by promoting women's rights, the protests would end. If not– if the president continued to stand in the way of women's equality– the Silent Sentinels would return.

 In early January, 1918, President Wilson astonished the nation by urging members of congress to pass the Susan B. Anthony Amendment. The House of Representatives passed the amendment on January 10, 1918. After much debate, and more protests, the Senate passed the same amendment in June 1919.

 Finally, after decades of difficult struggle and desperate dreams, women had secured for themselves the right to vote. We'll never know how many women throughout those years took part in this quest for freedom, how many women stood in front of the White House gates facing freezing temperatures, violent mobs, and the possibility of arrest. But we do know that because of their sacrifice our world has become a fairer place. Those women were not allowed to vote –they were not supposed to share their opinions or try to change the world– but they did it anyway. They took on a government that didn't want to hear their voices and they forced that government to change. In doing so, they gave all of us a great gift: a world with more freedom, equality, and respect.

Suffragists celebrate their victory.

Alice Paul celebrates.

EPILOGUE

We'll never know what happened to most of the Silent Sentinels. Many of them likely returned to their homes to raise families, work jobs, and live normal lives. In many ways these suffragists were not extraordinary people; they were ordinary women who chose to do an extraordinary thing. When their goal was accomplished, when they had succeeded at changing the world, they went back to their quiet lives, disappearing from the pages of history.

Some of them, though, continued their struggle for equality. They strove to help workers, both men and women, gain better conditions at their jobs and fairer wages for their labor. They worked to protect the rights of children and protested against warfare and the government's use of violence. Some of the suffragists continued their struggle for women's freedom. Alice Paul worked for women's equality throughout her entire life, traveling around the world, struggling to ensure that women could be treated as equals everywhere on the planet.

Our world is not a perfect place, and many problems still exist. But for every problem that is out there, there are people who work tirelessly trying to make things better. For these people who fight for peace and equality, the suffragists act as a sort of example. Though sometimes the road can seem hard, with enough dedication and sacrifice, even the most difficult obstacle can be conquered. In this way, the Sentinels' work is still happening. Those women's sacrifice is like a lighthouse, a brilliant flame reminding all of us that a better world is possible if we're willing to make it happen.

APPENDIX: FACES OF THE SENTINELS

Nobody knows how many women took time out of their lives to travel to Washington and join the Sentinels in their demonstrations in front of the White House. We do know that between the years 1917 and 1919 at least 168 suffragists were arrested and spent time in jail. These are the faces and names of just some of the women who were willing to sacrifice their freedom in order to make our world a better place.

Pauline Adams

Edith Ainge

Annie Arniel

The Suffragist Flag

Virginia Arnold

Abby Scott Baker

Lucy Gwynne Branham

Eunice Dana Brannan

Lucy Burns

Iris Calderhead

Gertrude Crocker

Julia Emory

Lucy Ewing

Catharine Flanagan

Janet Fotheringham

Matilda Hill Gardner

Betty Gram

Natalie Gray

Ernestine Hara

Kate Heffelfinger

Minnie Hennessy

Florence Bayard Hilles

Allison Turnbull Hopkins

Julia Hurlbut

Hazel Hunkins

Dora Lewis

Anne Martin

Vida Milholland

Agnes Morey

Katharine Morey

Mary Nolan

Alice Paul

Minnie Quay

Elizabeth Rogers

Nina Samarodin

Caroline Spencer

Doris Stevens

Elizabeth Stuyvesant

Mabel Vernon

Madeleine Watson

Helena Hill Weed

Anna Kelton Wiley

Rose Winslow

Joy Young

Matilda Young

REFERENCES

Beasley, Vanessa B. "Engendering Democratic Change: How Three U.S. Presidents Discussed Female Suffrage." *Rhetoric & Public Affairs* 5.1 (2002): 79-103. JSTOR. Web. 15 Jan. 2013.

Gallery of Suffrage Prisoners. Women of Protest: Photographs from the Records of the National Woman's Party, Manuscript Division, Library of Congress, Washington, D.C. http://www.loc.gov/collection/women-of-protest/articles-and-essays/gallery-of-suffrage-prisoners/ . Web. 20 Feb. 2014.

Gillmore, Inez Haynes. *The Story of the Woman's Party.* New York: Harcourt, Brace and Company, 1921. Google Books. Web. 1 Feb. 2013.

Hunter Graham, Sally. "WoodrowWilson, Alice Paul, and the Woman Suffrage Movement." *Political Science Quarterly* 98.4 (Winter 1983-1984): 665-679. JSTOR. Web. 15 Jan. 2013.

Lavender, William, and Mary Lavender. "Suffragists' Storm Over Washington." *American History* Oct. 2003: 30-35. JSTOR. Web. 15 Jan. 2013. McKee, Jim. "Clara Bewick and Women's Right to Vote in Nebraska." *Lincoln Journal Star* 7 Oct. 2012: F6. Print.

Stillion Southard, Belinda A. "Militancy, Power, and Identity: The Silent Sentinels as Women Fighting for Political Voice." *Rhetoric & Public Affairs* 10.3 (2007): 399-418. JSTOR. Web. 15 Jan. 2013.

Walton, Mary. *A Woman's Crusade.* New York: Palgrave Macmillan, 2010. Print.